Jainism

and

Jain Architecture

Ravish Kumar

B K Das

Copyright © 2018

First edition- 2018

ISBN: 978-1-387-50342-1

Published by: Lulu

Printed in USA

Preface

India is the originator of three principal religion Hinduism, Buddhism and Jainism. Hinduism belief on number of gods, Buddhism belief on Gautam Budha while Jainism Belief on twenty four Tirthankara. The objective of this books is to highlight the basic principal of Jain religion, their ethics and religious evolution in the form of Jain temple Architecture. An attempt have been made to correlate Jainism with the Jain Temple Architecture. A number of monument is existing thorought the country. Some of them with their Architecture features is tried to be incorporated as best example of Jain Architecture for which it is famous in the world. The explanation starts with the kandgiri – udaygiri cave dated about first century B.C. in the form of cave Architecture on the two hills, Khajuraho jain temple, Jal Mandir at Pawapuri, Mana Stambha, samvarsan Temple, Dilwara Temple, Parashnath hill etc. . All these placed of Jainism are famous on various grounds and presently of great interest worldwide due to its Architectural beauty.

TABLE OF CONTENTS

1.1 Introduction

In the Jain authoritative writings (called Agamas), the spellbinding word "Arhat" is joined with Lord Rishabh. The religion propounded by "Arhat" is known as 'Arhat dharma'. This is the out of date name of Jain religion. In out of date Vaidika composing, for instance, Padmapurana, Matsyapurana, Shiv purana thus on. We find the suggestion to Arhat dharma. The expression "Arhat" kept on being in vogue till Lord Parshvanath. Ruler Mahavir was more commonly known as 'Shraman Bhagwan'. In the midst of the period of Mahavir the word 'Nirgranth Pravachan' was in vogue in Jain religion. In the season of Mahavir and for two centuries after his freedom 'Nirgrantha Pravachan' remained inescapable. Later on in third and fourth century, the name 'Jain Religion' showed up. Mahavir being the rest of 24 Thirthankars, another example seemed to have set in and its followers there after called Jains. At present, the word 'Jain Religion' implies the aggregate custom and teachings of Thirthankars[1].

The announcing's of "Jin" is the foundation of 'Jain Religion'. One who has trust in preachings of "Jin" and who sharpens it is called Jain. As the Buddhist religion was sponsored by Buddha and the Christianity was sponsored by Jesus, so in like manner the religion

---

[1]Dutt, R. C. (1908) *Civilisation in the Buddhist Age*. Calcutta.

sponsored by Jin (Arhat) is called Jain Religion[2]. As the follower of Shiva is called 'Shaivs', the supporter of Vishnu is called Vaishnav, so furthermore the lover of "Jin" is called Jains. Christ, Shiva and Vishnu are close to home names. However, the expression "Jin" donot relate to any individual. Jain religion does not have confidence in loving a man. It venerates the certifiable attributes of a spirit who has achieved the condition of "Jin" i.e., who has destroyed the shroud of Karmas on learning, nature and vitality of soul[3].

Jains have 24 Tirthankars. The Jains finish their history the lives of 24 Tirthankars. According to Jain custom, Lord Rishabh was the essential middle person of Ahinsa (Non-brutality). Ruler Mahavir, predominantly seen as the originator of Jainism, was the rest of the Tirthankars who thrived from 599 to 527 B.C. So he could be known as a reformer of the Jain Religion or rejunevator of the certainty which was by then and had a long custom.[4]

---

[2]Dwivedi, O. P. (1989) *World Religions and the Environment.* New Delhi:Gitanjali Publishing House.

[3]Dwivedi, R. C. (ed) (1975) *Contribution of Jainism.* Banaras: Motilal Banarsidass.

[4]Eisenstadt, S. N. (1984) "Dissent, heterodoxy and civilisational Dynamics: some analytical and comparative indications", In Eisenstadt et al, (eds) *Orthodoxy, Heterodoxy and Dissent in India.* Berlin: Mouton.

The commitment of the primary Jain Tirthankar Rishabhadev is strengthening the Indian way can be apparant on four perspectives. Also, the first among them is that being an unimaginable and insightful caltivator he arranged Indians in think rural work. Getting the overall population the scope of straightforwardness was Rishbhdev's second genuine commitment.

Rishabh the essential Tirthankara set up the structure of direct dharma. The third and ever critical commitment of Rishabh towards the Indian way had been in his work and teachings of working up the art of house endeavors and that as well as demonstrated according to popular demand of time and space. In his relationship too, he arranged the general population. His fourth commitment had been in his examplary teachings of sensible dependability particularly for the individuals who were incorporated into business for their livlihood. All the over four commitments of Rishbhadev, notwithstanding being extra traditional willfully, justify giving a thought until today. Tirthankar Rishbhadev is ideal for the individuals who consider the Indian way, who are stressed of making thusly firm and broad in winning conditions of India and the whole world[5]. Unquestionably, in such way, Rishabhdev goes past the purposes of imprisonment set by a particular religious gathering.

---

[5]Eliade, Mircea (1961) *the Sacred and the Profane*. New York: Harper and Row.

Being a magnificent guide, elucidator and protect, Mahavir the 24th Tirthankar adopted the Indian strategies to statures. The Ratna-traya system set up by him is one of the living instances of it. Through Ratna-trya structure – Samyak darshan –samyak jnana and samyak charitra – he propelled the general population to proceed to accomplish the most vital period of humankind.[6]

1.2 Jain Philosophy

The Jain structure, like the Buddhist, is non-mysterious. It doesn't perceive the nearness of creator of God. Another fundamental component is that it is pluralistic system. The souls are various, unending in number. Moksha is not maintenance into the exceptional but instead the achievement of a faultless, splendid and blissed soul which is without body and without exercises.[7]

The religious rationale of Jainism demonstrates that there are nine truths or substances (Nav-tattva) They are : (1) soul (jiva) (2) non-soul (ajiva) (3) legitimize (punya) (4) sin or blame (daddy) (5) surge of Karma (asrava) (6) stoppage of karmic matter (Samvara) (7)

---

[6]Eliot, Charles (1962) *Hinduism and Buddhism*, vol. I. London: Routledge and Kegan Paul.

[7]Flügel, Peter (2000) "Protestantische und Post-Protestantische Jaina-Reformbewegungen: Zur Geschichte und Organisation der Sthanakavasi" I. *Berliner Indologische Studien* 13/14: 37-103.pp.

oppression (bandha) (8) shedding of karmic matter (nirjara) and (9) opportunity (moksha).

1. Jiva (soul): The standard of Jiva is a mindful substance which is differing in different individuals. The amount of Jivas (souls) is unending. The spirit is not quite recently the enjoyer of the results of karma (bhokta), furthermore the performing craftsman, significantly possessed with wordly undertakings and responsible for his showing (karma), awesome or horrendous. It transmigrates i.e., it takes dynamic births as demonstrated by the method for heap of its deeds. It can accomplish freedom (moksha) from the cycle of birth and going by freeing itself from all that is non-soul (ajiva), by pulverizing collected karmas and by stopping their further merging into it.

2. Ajiva (non-soul): Ajiva is the backwards of jiva including dharma, adharma, akash, pudgala and kala substances, of these, the underlying three (medium of development, medium of rest, space or medium of settlement are vague (amurta) and bound together wholes. The forward substance matter is described as what is head of the qualities of touch, taste, shading and smell. Time is atomic in estimation and the kala particles invade the whole gigantic space.

3.   Punya (authenticity): Punya is the consequence of good and religious deeds. There are nine ways to deal with it. They are, truth is told, assorted sorts of practicing magnanimity.

4.   Papa (sin or negative check): It is called sin or severe dislike, is an essential issue in the oppression of jiva. Mischief to and butchering of living-creatures is a miserable sin and brings about stunning discipline[8].

5.   Asrava (meeting of karma): Asrava connotes the inflow of karmic matter by the spirit. Correspondingly as water streams into a watercraft through an opening, so the karmic matter travels through asrava into the spirit. The method for activity is shubha (commendable) or ashubha (demeritorious). The rule "like causes make like results" is recognized as a choosing component of the Jain teaching of karma[9].

6.   Samvara (stoppage of karmic matter): Samvara infers ending, controlling or halting of inflow of karmic matter

---

[8]Flügel, Peter (2003) "The Code of Conduct of the Terapanth Saman Order", *South Asia Research* 23(1): 7-53.

[9]Flügel, Peter (2006) "Jainism and Society", *Bulletin of SOAS* 68: 91-112.

into the spirit, smavara is influenced through balance (gupti), constrained advancement (samiti), standards (dharma), examination (anupreksha), triumph of hardship and religious lead.

7. Bandha (enslavement): Bandha is the union of jiva with pudgala (matter) or soul with non-soul particles. The matter is controlled by five causes, to be particular wrong conviction, association, imprudence, interests and movement.

8. Nirjara (shedding the karmic matter): Nirjara suggests shedding off, leaving or demolition. Nirjara is to wreck and burnup amassed karma. Take the instance of a tank. By stopping the inflow of water into the tank, we catch the development of water in the tank. That is samvara, yet there is starting at now some water in the tank. Remembering the true objective to leave this water, it may be displayed to the glow of the sun for a long time. This is nirjara.

9. Moksha (opportunity): Moksha is the exceptional period of supernatural accomplishment when all reasons for subjugation having been expelled; the spirit is freed from karmic matter. It is a period of peace, immaculate certainty, romanticizes data, and a period of having achieved siddhi. Moksha is accomplished however right certainty, right data

and right direct. For the perfection of right lead, five kind of guarantees prescribed: Non-brutality (ahinsa), honesty (satya), non-taking (asteya), chastity (brahmacharya) and no insatiability (aparigraha).

1.3 Karma Philosophy

The word has two ramifications, one is 'any activity' and other is fine particles that get pulled in and stick to the spirit because of its movement. That which is being done is "karma" is the authentic foundation of the term karma. Both these suggestions are fitting in the one of a kind condition. The whole universe is loaded down with fine karmic particles. In any case, when these particles get pulled into the spirit and stick to it and tie it through its activity, then just they are doled out by the term karma.

The karmic particles bound with the spirit are called, "dravya karma" or physical karma while inward conditions of association, loathing are visitor 'bhava karma' or mental karma. In a manner of speaking Jains perceive mental are extraordinary karma. The spirit (ordinary soul) is the expert of both these karmas. They are regularly related as conditions and final products, comparably as a seed and a tree. It can be said when I am associated with something I would do negative karmas, the karmic particles related with the karma would then get bound with my spirit and make me experience the products of my exercises later. In non-Jain course of action of philosophy the going with words are used for karma: In vedanta it is maya, avidya and prakriti, in Mimansa it is apurva, in Buddhist and Yoga it is vasna, in Sankhya and Yoga it is asaya, in Nayaya and Vaishesika it is dharmadharam, adrsta and sanskar.

(i) Cause of enslavement: The karmic material particles are first pulled into the spirit and a while later bound by it. The limit of attracting them to the spirit is performed by the movement of mind, talk and body. So the movement is called asrava (immersion), rather reason for surge and the limit of restricting the karmic particles with the spirit is performed by mithyatva (unwholesome inclination or certainty or conviction), avirti (non-control), pramada (slowness) and kasaya (vitality). So they are known as the road of bondage. Every movement that is there with these four goes about as a reason for subjugation. Yoga or movement alone is called asrava, the remaining four like kasaya or not asrava or merging but instead the reasons for asrava. From this we can appreciate that yoga (movement) is the reason for both the immersion and the oppression.

(ii) Philosophy of rebirth: Every birth of a spirit is rebirth in context of its past birth. There can never be any birth which is not related with the past birth. The course of action of soul's birth has no begin. In the event that we by one means or another happened to expect that a spirit is borne shockingly, then it would induce that it is possible that even a perfect soul that has freed itself from the birth-cycle by virtue of its accomplishment of flawlessness ought to take birth eventually.

9

This would render endless, out and out and admire opportunity unfathomable. It would be senseless to trust that the spirit remains free from birth for eventually starts to expect birth yet again. It is sensible to hold that the course of action of birth continues, in case it goes before by any extend of the creative ability, without interruption and that once it is snapped; it is snapped until the end of time.

As indicated by conviction of Jain religion freedom is described as, "Correspondingly as the oil plant is attempted to separate oil from sesamum seeds, blending is grasped to separate ghee from margarine deplete and fire is used to separate metal from metal, so in like manner the spirit achieves freedom reparation through and restriction."

1.4   Jain Traditions

Indian culture can be characterized into two general social affairs – (1) Brahaman (Vedic) culture (2) Shraman culture. The philosophical school of Mimansa, Vedanta, Nyaya and Vaishesika fall into top of the line. The philosophical schools of Jain, Buddhist and Sankhya have a place with the Shraman culture

The custom of Jain philosophy and Tirthankars is to a great degree old. I am particularly of the view that Jain philosophy is Sanatan; confirmations of nearness of Tirthankar Rishabhdev have been found in tunneling work of goals of the Indus valley human advancement. Not only was this, as per the predetermined Jain treatises, Rishbhdev, the essential Tirthankar, was the son of Nabhi and Marudevi, the ruler and leader of Ayodhya. In the Rig-veda itself he has been determined as one of the Avatars-incarnations. In treatises of Hindus and Jains both it has moreover been indicated that Rishbhadev was from Ikshavasu family. Particularly Jain treatises descirbe that Hindustan (India) was known as Bharat due to Bharat, the eldest son of Rishbhadev and who was a wonderful ruler. Point of fact, the Jain convention is extremely old. Like Hinduism history of Jainism is old. Along these lines, from antiquated conditions and particularly from the season of Tirthankar Rishbhadev, Jainism has contributed phenomenally towards strengthening and working up the Indian way.

1.5   Thirthankars

Jainism is the old religion of India and in the midst of its long and unbroken nearness it is proclaimed by 24 Great Preachers known as "Jinas" i.e. "Vanquishers" or "Tirthankaras" i.e. 'Fordmakers over the surge of nearness'. These 24 Tirthankaras are:

1.   **Shree Aadinath**

2.   **Shree Ajitnath**

3.   **Shree Aambhav nath**

4.   **Shree Abhinandana nath**

5.   **Shree Sumati nath**

11

6. Shree Padamprabhu

7. Shree Suparshva nath

8. Shree Chandra prabhu

9. Shree Pushpadant

10. ShreeShital nath

11. Shree Shreyans nath

12. Shree Vasupujya

13. Shree Vimal nath

14. Shri Anant nath

15. Shree Dharm nath

16. Shree Shanti nath

17. Shree Kunthu nath

18. Shree Arah nath

19. Shree Malli nath

20. Shree Munisuvrata nath

21. Shree Nami nath

22. Shree Nemi nath

23. ShreeParshav nath

24. Shree Mahavira

Along these lines the tradition of Tirthankaras begins with Rishabha, the primary Tirthankara, and terminations with Mahavira, the twentyfourth Tirthankara. Really, there is a reliable association among these twenty-four Tirthankaras who thrived in different circumstances of history in India. It in this way suggests the religion at first lectured by Rishabha in the remote past was lectured by the progression of remaining twenty-three Tirthankaras in the midst of their life-time for the benefit of living creatures.[10] In context of this progression of twenty-four Tirthankaras well-weave intelligibility is kept up both in the principles and practices of Jaina religion. Since Mahavira is the twenty-fourth Tirthankara in this line of Tirthankaras, he, by no means whatsoever, could be considered as the originator of Jaina religion. From this time forward Mahavira is not the creator yet rather the promulgator and unprecedented evangelist of Jaina religion in the midst of the sixth century B.C. As Mahavira happens to be the last Tirthankara, he is seen by the normal people as the creator of Jaina religion. Unmistakably this is a confused judgment. By and by it has been a recognized conviction by the antiquarians that Mahavira did not found Jaina religion but instead he lectured the religion which was in nearness from the remote past.

---

[10]Flügel, Peter (ed) (2006) *Studies in Jain History and Culture: Disputes and Dialogues.* London: Routledge.

1.6 Trustworthiness of the Jaina Tradition

The Historicity of this Jaina tradition is adequately borne one both by aesthetic and archeological affirmations.In the beginning of the twentieth century various scholars were under the inclination that Maiaavira was a whimsical or an amazing figure. A little while later they comprehended that Mahavira was a recorded figure yet they trusted that Malaavira and Gautama Buddha are the two names of a comparative person, viz. Gautama Buddha. Early looks at in the twentieth century scattered this perplexity about Mahavira and Gautama Buddha and set up an alternate and differing personality of Mahavira. Consequently however Mahavira's veritable and free nearness was recognized; still he was seen as the coordinator of Jaina religion and as the champion of quietness who opposed the awful practices of Brahmanism. The present investigates in chronicled and indological contemplates finished by Western and Oriental Scholars have emptied certain the considerations of past journalists about the piece of Mahavira and have now completely settled the way that Mahavira is not the coordinator of Jaina religion yet rather the promulgator of Jaina religion which was in inescapability in India, especially in Eastern India from the old past. This view is evidently expressed by P. C. Roy Chaudhury in his book `Jainism in Bihar' in the going with terms: "A run of the mill oversight has been made by a part of the present authors in holding that Jainism was imagined because of discontent against Brahmanism. This wrong hypothesis begins in light of the way that

14

these essayists have taken Vardhamana Mahavira as the writer of Jainism. This is not a reality. The belief had starting at now began and spread and Mahavira multiplied it inside important conditions."

Accordingly it is as of now a recognized fact that Mahavira is the Tirthankara or prophet of Jaina religion and that he lectured the religion which was broadcasted in the eighth Century B.C. by his forerunner Parshvanatha, the 23rdTirthankara. The precision of Parshvanatha (877-777 B.C.) has been unmistakably settled. Parshvanatha, the son of King Vishvasena and Queen Vamadevi of Kingdom of Kashi, drove the life of a stark, practiced genuine requital, gained omniscience, transformed into a Tirthankara, multiplied Jaina religion and accomplished Nirvana or salvation when he was 100 years of age at Sammet Shikhara, i.e. Parasnatha slant in Hazaribag District of Bihar State. Parshavanatha as often as possible gets the sobriquet 'a charming or warm personality'. His understudies like Kesikumara occupied the season of Mahavira and held minor complexities in shut disapproved of unpretentious components however the fundamental religious belief framework was in a general sense the same as that of Mahavira. Unmistakable students of history like Vincent Smith, R.C. Majumdar, and R.K. Mookarji see Parshvanatha as a real personage and an unprecedented clergyman of Jaina religion.

The predecessor of Parshvanatha was Nemi-natha or Arishtanemi, the 22nd Tirthankara and the dependability of Nemi-natha like that of Parshvanatha, could be easily settled. Nemi-natha was the certified cousin of the observed Lord Krishna of Mahabharata as Samudravijaya, the father - of Neini-natha, and Vasudeva, the father of Krishna, were kin. Nemi-natha had a unique personality in view of his wonderful sensitivity towards animals. This is unmistakably revealed by asignificant event in his life. While Nemi-natha was proceeding at the pioneer of his wedding parade to the place of his woman of great importance, Princess Rajulakumari, the girl of King Ugrasena, he heard the moans and groans of animals put in a walled in area for some meat-eaters and in a brief moment picked not to marry at all as his marriage would incorporate such a butcher of such an expansive number of guiltless animals. In a split second Nemi-natha renounced his magnificent title and transformed into a self-denying. Leaving this renunciation of Nemi-natha, the promised princess Rajulakumari or Rajamati also transformed into a house follower and entered the self-denying demand. Nemi-natha lectured religion for a significant extended period of time in conclusion achieved Nirvana on the Mount Girnar, in Junagadha District of Gujrat State. As Nemi-natha denied the world, he didn't share in the personal clash of Malaabharata like his cousin kin Lord Krishna. Since this Great War of Mahabharata must be acknowledged as a historical event and Krishna to be a historical personage, then his cousin kin Nemi-natha is furthermore met all requirements for have a place in this historical picture.There is in like manner an inscriptional affirmation to show the reliability of Nemi-natha. Dr. Pran Nath dispersed in the "Seasons of India" (dated 19thMarch 1935) a copperplate surrender of the Babylonian King

Nebuchadnazzar I (1140 B. C.) found at Prabhaspattan in Gujrat State, which, as demonstrated by his examining, suggests the Babylonian King having come to Mount Revet to pay respect to Lord Nemi-rlatha. Dr. Fuherer also announced on the commence of Mathura Jaina old pieces that Nemiriatha was a historical personage (vide Epigraphia Indica, I, and II, 208-210). Propel, we find Nemi-natha's photos of the Indo-Scythian period bearing inscriptions determining his name. These are various distinctive etchings bolster the exactness of 22nd Tirthankara Nemi-natha.

Among whatever is left of the 21 Tirthankaras of the Jaina tradition, there are a couple references from different sources to the key Tirthankara Rishabhanatha or Adinatha. Subsequently the tradition of twenty-four Tirthankaras is determinedly settled among the Jainas and what is genuinely superb about this Jaina tradition is the certification of it from non-Jaina sources, especially Buddhist and Hindu sources.

1.7 Jaina Belief and Buddhism

Mahavira was the senior contemporary of Gautama Buddha the originator of Buddhism, in the Buddhist writing there are a couple references of a personal kind of Mahavira. Regardless, it is to a great degree gigantic to note that in Buddhist books Mahavira is continually delineated as Nigantha Nataputta (Nirgrantha Jnatriputra, i.e., the stripped stark of the Jnatr tribe) and never as the originator of Jainism. Advance in the Buddhist writing Jainism is not showed up as another religion but instead is implied as an antiquated religion. There are satisfactory references in Buddhist books to Jaina uncovered religious severity, to love af.Arhats in Jaina Chaityas or sanctuaries and to the Chaturyama Dharma (i.e. fourfold religion) of 23rd Tirthankara Parshvanatha.

Furthermore it is outstandingly suitable to find that the Buddhist writing insinuates the Jaina tradition of Tirthankaras and especially indicates the names of Jaina Tirthankaras like Rishabhadeva, Padmaprabha, Chandprabha, Pushpadanta, Vimala-natha, Dharma-natha and Nemi-natha. The 'Dharmottarapradipa', the remarkable Buddhist book, sees Rishabhadeva close by the name of Mahavira or Vardhamana as an Apta or Tirthankara. The "Dhammikasutta" of the 'Anguttra Nikaya' discusses Arishtanemi or nemi-natha as one of the six Tirthankaras. The Buddhist book 'Manoratha-Purani", sees the names of numerous laymen and women as aficionados of Parshvanatha tradition and among them is the name of Vappa, the uncle of Gautama Buddha. To be sure it is determined that Gautama Buddha himself practiced compensation as shown by the Jaina system before he propounded his new religion.

Propel, it is basic to note that the names and amounts of Buddhas, Paccekabuddhas and Bodhisattvas in Buddhism appear to have been affected by those of the Jaina Tirthankaras. For instance, Ajita, the name of the second Jaina Tirthankaras, has been given to one Paccekabuddha. Padma, the 6th Jaina Tirthankara, is the name of the eighth of the 24 Buddhas. Vimala, a Paccekabuddha, has been named after Vimala-Natha, the thirteenth Jaina Tirtliankara.

1.8 Jaina Belief and Hinduism

The Jaina tradition of 24 Tirthankaras seems to have been recognized by the Hindus, like the Buddhists, as could be seen from their old consecrated writings. The Hindus, without a doubt, never scrutinized the way that Jainism was established by Rishabhadeva and put his time about at what they envisioned to be the start of the world. They remembered him as a magnificent person and numbered him among their Avataras i.e. distinctive incarnations of Lord Vishnu. They give a comparative parentage (father Nabhiraja and mother Marudevi) of Rishabhadeva as the Jainas do and they even agree that after the name of Rishabhadeva's eldest son Bharata this country is known as Bharata-Varsha. [11]

So far as the most seasoned Vedic writing is concerned justifiesthat this term alludes to Rishabhadeva, who could be considered as the immense pioneer of the Vratyas.

In the later Puranic literature of the Hindus likewise there are abundant references to Rishabhadeva. The account of Rishabha

---

[11]Flügel, Peter (2007) "A Short History of Jain Law," *Jaina Studies Newsletter*, 2: 24-27.

happens in the Vishnupurana and Bhagavata-Purana, where he figures as an Avatara i.e. incarnation of Narayana, during a time before that of ten avataras of Vishnu. The story is precisely identical with the life-history of Rishabhadeva'sgiven in the Jaina consecrated literature. Thusly, Rishabhadeva's life and critical significance described in the Jaina literature get affirmed by the account of Rishabha given in the Hindu Puranas. Thusly from the way that Hindu tradition regards Rishabha-devaand not Mahavira-close by Gautama Buddha as an incarnion of God, one may state that the Hindu tradition also recognizes Rishabhadeva as the coordinator of Jainism.

1.9 Jaina Tradition and Archeological Evidence

From some historical references it can be regarded that Rishabhadeva, must be the honest to goodness coordinator of Jainism. In this affiliation Dr. Jacobi forms in like manner, "There is nothing to exhibit that Parshva was the coordinator of Jainism. Jaina tradition is reliable in making Rishabla, the essential Tirthankara as its originator and there may be something historical in the tradition which makes him the main Tirthankara". There is affirmation to exhibit that so far back as the essential century B.C. there were individuals who were revering Rishabhadeva. It has been recorded

20

that Kin of Kalinga in his second interruption of Magadha in 161 B.C. brought back treasures from Magadha and in these treasures there was the statue of the essential Jaina (Rishabhadeva) which had been occupied from Kalinga three centuries earlier by King Nanda I.This infers that in the fifth Century B.C. Rishabhadeva was revered and his statue was astoundingly regarded by his adherents. From this it is found that if Mahavira or Parshvanatha were the coordinators of Jainism, then their statues would have been loved by their devotees in the fifth Century B.C, i.e. rapidly after their time. Regardless, as we get in old inscriptions true blue historical references to the statues of Rishabhadeva it can be insisted that he almost certainly been the coordinator of Jainism.

Other archeological affirmations having a place with the Indus Valley Civilization of the Bronze Age in India moreover credit support to the matured relic of the Jaina tradition and prescribe the inescapability of the act of love of Rishabhadeva, the lst Tirthankara, nearby the love of various divinities. The current uncovering at Mohenjo-Daro and Harappa have revealed the honest to goodness nearness of a particularly all around made Pre-Vedic and non-Aryan Civilization known as the Indus Valley Civilization. Subsequently, history of India can now be taken after back to the Indus Valley Period (i.e. around 3500 to B.C.) and not upto the Vedic period (i.e. around 1500 to 1000 B.C.) similarly as was being done in the past. Frankly the current researches have exhibited that there is a characteristic connection between the Indus Valley Culture and the present day Indian Culture. It is particularly identified with note that various relics from the Indus Valley unearthings suggest the prevalence of Jaina religion in that most antiquated period.

1. It is watched that in the Indus Valley Civilization there is a wonderful predominance of earthenware figures of female divinities over these of male gods and that the figures of male gods are exhibited uncovered.in such way Dr. True Mackay, the prestigious Archeologist personally connected with the Indus Valley uncovering, sees that "For reasons obscure which it is difficult to fathom, figures of male divinities in ceramics are unmistakably unprecedented: They are out and out bare, on the other hand with the female figures, which ceaselessly wear a touch of clothing; bits of adornments and bangles, may be worn, however this is by no means whatsoever, constantly the case". This truth evidently reveals the indications of Jaina religion among the Indus Valley individuals as the love of bare male gods is an uncommonly settled practically speaking in Jaina religion.

2. Further, the figures engraved on the seals found in the uncovering also prescribe a comparative thing. For example, we find that the figures of six male divinities fit as a fiddle are engraved on one seal (Vide Sir John Marshall: Mohanjo-Daro and the Indus Civilization,and that each figure is indicated exposed and standing erect in a

mulling over temperament with both the hands keeping near the body). Since this `Kayotsarga' way (i.e. in standing stance) rehearsing penance is curious just to the Jainas and the figures are of exposed ascetics, it can be kept up that these figures speak to the Jaina Tirthankaras.

3. Again, the figures of male deities in pondering inclination and in sitting field engraved on the seals (Vide Sir John Marshall: Mohanjo- Daro and the Indus Civilization), look like the figures of Jaina Tirthankaras in light of the fact that in these, the male deities are delineated as having one face just while the figures of male deities, expected to be the prototypes of Lord Shiva, are for the most part portrayed as having three confront, three eyes and three horns. (vide Sir John Marshall: Mohanjo-Daro and the Indus Civilization)

4. Moreover, on a couple seals we find the figure of a bull engraved underneath the figure of an uncovered male heavenly nature sharpening atonement in the "Kayotsarga" way i.e. in a standing position. These figures appear, in every way, to be the depictions of Rishabhadeva, the 1st Jaina Tirthankara, as a result of the truths that among the 'Jainas there is a developed practice of portraying the Lanchhana i.e. the token of each Tirthankara underneath his divinity and that the symbol of Rishabhadeva is bull.

5. Likewise, the heavenly indications of Swastika are found engraved on different seals. It is pertinent to note that the Swastika signs engraved on Seals Nos. 502, 503, 506 and 514 definitely take after the set up Jaina practice of drawing Swastika signs.

6. Further, there are a couple subjects on the seals found in Mohanjo-Daro and it is suggested that these topics are indistinguishable with those found in the antiquated Jaina art of Mathura.

From this archeological confirmation it can be expressed that there are insights of love of Jaina divinities and that there was the pervasiveness of love of Jaina Tirthankara Rishabhadeva alongwith the love of Hindu God who is believed to be the model of Lord Shiva in the Indus Valley Civilization. This nearness of Jaina tradition in the most punctual time of Indian history is supported by various scientists like Dr. Radha Kumud Mookarji, Gustav Roth, Prof. A. Chakravarti, Prof. Crush Prasad Whanda, T.N. Ramchandran, Champat Rai Jain, Kamta Prasad Jain and Dr. Pran Nath.

Regarding remnant of Jaina tradition of Tirthankaras Major J.G.R. Forlong (in his books 'Short-looks at in the Science of Comparative Religion') forms that from cloud conditions there existed in India an exceedingly dealt with Jaina religion from which later on made Brahmanism and Buddhism and that Jainism was lectured by twenty-two Tirthankaras before the Aryans accomplished the Ganges. Dr Nmmerman moreover unequivocally supports the remnant of Jaina tradition in the going with terms. "There is truth in the Jaina believed that their religion retreats to remote remnant, the relic being alluded to being that of the Pre-Aryan. Jaina and Vedic Religions Traditions:

The remnant of Jaina religious tradition can in this way be taken after back to the timeliest time of Indian history. This Jaina tradition is Pre-Vedic and additionally. Obviously the Jaina religion was flourishing in India, especially in the eastern locales of India, where the Aryans came besides, theysettled in India. Thus from the happening to Aryans in India, we find the pervasiveness of two specific religious traditions in India, viz. the Vedic and the Jaina religious traditions. It is true that as a result of their major differences in precepts and practices of religion, these, two traditions were against each other and that each tradition attempted to charge the other. Notwithstanding this fight we see that both the traditions ran parallel in India, on occasion one getting the opportunity to be overwhelming and from time to time the other.

In the Vedic tradition the priest had a pre-well known position as he was the champion of ceremony. He vigorously attested that the welfare and point of fact the very nearness of the world, including even the Gods, depended on the upkeep of their frameworks of surrender, which created to monstrous size and desrve quality. The religions advanced by him were polytheistic; the divinities were as often as possible the qualities of nature; and man was put, at their expressive tolerance, the priest alone being prepared for saving him by searching for the support of the gods through mollifying traditions. This school of accepted was more discernible first in North-West India as the Aryans beginning from outside settled first in that area; however later on it spread towards the Eastern and Southern areas of India.

On the other hand in the Jaina tradition recognizable position was apportioned to the austere. In the Eastern district of India and especially along the productive banks of the Ganges and the Jamuna, there prospered a progression of austere Teachers, who, hailing from rich families, had enough amusement for high considering and religious meditation. For them, the spirit in man and moreover in each and every animate being, was the convergence of religious meditation and also a challenge of examination in association with all that is dormant in the universe. This passed on them eye to eye with the issue of life here and elsewhere, since both soul and matter were real for them-real, and thus fundamentally perpetual, however experiencing the flux of advance. Life here and consequently was the result of the starting less association among soul and matter, which was the wellspring of all the wretchedness in this world; and the purpose of religion was to separate matter from soul, so that the last may achieve a condition of opportunity in which it would exist in a plentitude of faultlessness, euphoria and learning[12]. Man is his own particular master; his contemplations, words and the exhibitions have made him, and continue making him, what he is; it is in his grip to make or imperfection his present or future; the monster Teachers of the past are his measures to propel him en route of religion; and he needs to fight with desire, on the well-trodden method for significant progress, after a code of good and parsimonious prepare, till he accomplishes the goal of otherworldly freedom or faultlessness[13].

In context of this belief framework there is no place, in the Jaina religious idea, either for a Deity who shape the universe and meddles in its matters, or for a priest contributed with mysterious powers to pacify that Deity. This line of accepted is continuosly and commandingly spoken to by Jaina Tirthankaras proper from Rishabhadeva to Mahavira. Later on a tantamount line of accepted was grasped by Ajivika Teachers like Gosala, by Sankhya Philosophers like Kapila and promulgators of Buddhism like Buddha.As these acidic Teachers of different religions and factions speak to for all intents and purposes a comparative line of thought; they are said to have a place with one far reaching tradition known as Shramana Tradition. Regularly the Jainas are the most settled delegates of Shramana tradition and Mahavira was the last among

---

[12]Flügel, Peter (2008) "The Unknown Lonka: Tradition and the Cultural Unconscious", pp. 181-271, in Caillat, Colette and Nalini

[13] Balbir (eds) *JainaStudies*. Delhi: Motilal Banarsidass.

the Jaina Tirthankaras who cleared up the tradition for the benefit of living beings.

1.10 Interesting Jainism Facts

➢ In Jainism all life has a spirit, from microorganisms to plants, to creatures and to humans. Since they all have souls they all can achieve nirvana.

➢ Jains don't worship a god or holy person, and rather work to accomplish nirvana as they believe other freed souls have attained.

➢ In Jainism the belief is that karma is really matter that appends to the spirit therefore of thoughts, actions, and words, paying little heed to whether they are sure or negative.

➢ In Jainism there is the belief that there are various universes. This is Bharat Kshetra, one of three universes that we might be reawakened into.

➢ In Jainism the swastika holds distinctive significance than what most connect it with (Nazis). The four areas each speak to one of the four states of presence (loathsome beings, plants/creatures, magnificent beings, humans). From birth until death humans can go through these brief states of being.

➢ Jains are veggie lovers due to their peaceful beliefs. They may likewise progress toward becoming veggie lover to keep away from the harm and decimation of current cultivating.

➤ Most Jains don't eat mushrooms, nectar, or root vegetables. They likewise don't drink liquor or take tranquilizes that modify the psyche.

➤ Fasting is regular in Jainism.

➤ Some outrageous Jains quick to death. These Jains like to bite the dust as opposed to make any agony the plants that they would somehow or another need to expend to survive.

➤ Jains make up India's most instructed religious gathering.

➤ In America Jains make up a portion of the wealthiest people in the nation.

➤ Jains make five pledges of restraint including Ahimsa (peacefulness), Satya (honesty), Asteya (no taking), Aparigraha (non-attachment), and Brahmacarya (pure living).

➤ In Jainism there are five sorts of learning including sensory information, scriptural learning, perceptiveness, clairvoyance, and omniscience.

➢ Jainism teaches that there are six basic substances including soul, matter, time, space, adharma, and dharma.

➢ Jainism alludes to the spirit substance as Jiva. The other five substances are alluded to as ajiva.

➢ In August or September Jains hold their most essential celebration called Paryushana, or Daslakshana. Amid this 8-10 day celebration Jains regularly quick, ruminate, and stress the five fundamental promises of restraint.

➢ Most Jains live in India where their population is believed to be between 4-6 million. Jain gatherings can be found in Europe, the United States, Kenya, and in Canada.

Chapter -2

2.1   Jainism in Bihar

Jainism in Bihar takes after a long history since the seasons of twenty-fourth Tirthankara Mahavira, who was born in Vaishali (close Patna). An antiquated dull statue of Lord Mahavira weighing around 250 kg was starting late stolen from Jamui, Bihar.[14] The statue was later recovered by the Police. Vasupujya; the twelfth Jain Tirthankara was born in Champapur, Bhagalpur. He achieved all his Pancha Kalyanaka (Garbha, Janma, Tapa, Kevala Jnana and Moksha) from Champapur. Vardhamana Mahavira, the 24th and the last Tirthankara of Jainism, was born in Vaishali around sixth century B.C.

Jain journeys in Bihar

Rajgir (initially known as Girivraj) is a city and a prompted region in Nalanda district in the Indian state of Bihar. The city of Rajgir (old Rājagṛha; Pali: Rājagaha; Hindi: राजगृह) was the essential capital of the kingdom of Magadha, an express that would at last form into the Mauryan Empire. Its date of birthplace is dark, disregarding the way that stoneware dating to around 1000 BC has been found in the city. This domain is moreover unmistakable in Jainism and

---

[14]Fohr, Sherry E. (2001) *Gender and Chastity: Female Jain Renouncers.* Ph.D.Thesis. University of Virginia.

32

Buddhism as one of the most loved spots for Lord Mahavira and Gautama Buddha and the outstanding "Atanatiya" meeting was held at Vulture's Peak Mountain.

History

The name Rajgir started from Rājagṛiha 'place of the master' or "celebrated house", or the word rajgir may have its cause in its plain demanding implying, "great mountain". It was the old capital city of the Magadha masters until the fifth century BC when Udayin (460-440 BC), son of Ajatshatrumoved the capital to Pataliputra. Back then, it was called Rajgrih, which decodes as 'the home of Royalty'. Shishunaga set up Shishunaga tradition in 413 BCE with Rajgir as its hidden capital before it was moved to Pataliputra.

Rajgir is in like manner surely understood for its association with Mauryan line Kings Bimbisara and Ajatashatru. Ajatashatru kept his father Bimbsara in bondage here. The sources don't agree which of the Buddha's great counterparts, Bimbisara and Ajatashatru was responsible for its improvement. Ajatashatru is furthermore ascribed with moving the capital to Pataliputra (Presently Patna).

The epic Mahabharata calls it Girivraja and depict the story of its ruler, Jarasandha, and his battle with the Pandava kin and their accomplices Krishna. Jarasandha, who hailed from this place, had been vanquished by Krishna 17 times. The eighteenth time Krishna left the battle zone without battling. Due to this Krishna is in like manner called "ranachorh" (one who has left the front line). Mahabharata relates a wrestling match between Bhima (one of the Pandavas) and Jarasandha, the then master of Magadha. Jarasandha was solid as his body could rejoin any disassembled members. According to the legend, Bhim split Jarasandha into two and hurled the two sections going up against converse to each other so they couldn't join. There is a well known Jarasandha's Akhara (put where hand to hand battling is practiced). It is in like manner said in Jain and Buddhist sacred texts, which give a movement of place-names, however without land setting. The attempt to discover these spots is building to a great extent concerning reference to them and to various territories in advance of Chinese Buddhist pioneers, particularly Fahian and Xuanzang. It is on the preface of Xuanzang particularly that the site is secluded into Old and New Rajgir. The past exists in a valley and is included by low-lying hills, Rajgir hills. It is portrayed by an earthen bank (the Inner Fortification), with which is connected the Outer Fortification, a complex of cyclopean dividers that keeps running (with vast breaks) along the pinnacle of the hills. New Rajgir is portrayed by another, bigger, dam outside the northern section of the valley and alongside the front line town. It was here that Gautama Buddha spent a while thinking about, and addressing at Gridhra-kuta, ('Hill of the Vultures'). He in like manner passed on some of his outstanding sermons and began ruler Bimbisara of Magadha and endless others to Buddhism. On one of the hills is the Saptparni surrender where the First Buddhist Council was held under the organization of Maha Kassapa.

It is heavenly to the memory of the originators of both the religions: Jainism and Buddhism and related with both the unquestionable Mahavira and Buddha.

Ruler Mahavira, 24th Tirthankara put in fourteen years of his life at Rajgir and Nalanda, spending Chaturmas (i.e. 4 months of the tempestuous season) at a solitary place in Rajgir (Rajgruhi) and the rest in the spots in the area. It was the capital of one of his Shravaks (follower) King Shrenik. Appropriately Rajgir is a basic religious place for Jains. The twentieth Jain tirthankara, Munisuvrata ought to have been born here. An antiquated temple (about 1200 years old) dedicated to Munisuvrat bhagwan is in like manner present here close by various other jain sanctuaries. This sanctuary is furthermore a place for four Kalyanakas of Bhagwan Munisuvratnath.

2.2 Jainism in Jharkhand

Shikharji (Śikharjī), Giridih territory, Jharkhand, India, is arranged on Parasnath, the most elevated mountain of the Parasnath Range. It is a Jain Tirtha (journey site) accepted to be the place twenty of the twenty-four Jain tirthankaras close by various diverse monks achieved Moksha, according to Nirvana Kanda and distinctive writings

Historical background

Shikharji infers the "regarded zenith". The site is furthermore called Sammed Śikhar or Sammet Shikhar "zenith of focus" since it is a place where twenty of twenty-four Tirthankaras achieved Moksha. "Parasnath" is gotten from Parshvanatha, the twenty-third tirthankara, who was one of the individuals who is accepted to have accomplished Moksha at the site.

Geology

Shikarji is arranged in an inland bit of provincial east India. It lies on NH-2, the Delhi-Kolkata expressway in a zone called the Grand Trunk Street. Shikharji rises to 4,429 feet (1,350 m) making it the most elevated mountain in Jharkhand state

History

The most dependable reference to Shikharji as a tirth (place of journey) is found in the Jñātṛdhārmakātha, one of the twelve focus writings of Jainism: at Shikharji, Māllīnātha, the nineteenth tirthankara, practiced samadhi. Shikharji is furthermore said in the Pārśvanāthacarita, a twelfth century record of Pārśva.

The pervasiveness of Shikharji as a site of journey took after that of Vulture Peak, Bihar, where it is trusted the Buddhist Sariputta achieved enlightenment.

Jharkhand acquired Shikharji under the Bihar Land Reforms Act, leaving the benefits of Jains in vulnerability. Use of Shikharji as a vacationer objective furthermore impacts on the religious beliefs of the Jain. Diversions, for instance, paragliding and parasailing may occur at Shikharji.

Approach

The journey to Shikharji is a round outing of 30 km through the Madhuban woods. The zone from Gandharva Nala stream to the summit is the most blessed to Jains. The journey is made by strolling or by a litter or doli passed on by a doliwallah along a strong cleared track. Along the track are asylums to each of the twenty four tirthankaras and shippers of tea, coffee, water, verdant sustenances.

There is Some Possibility that parikrama of the entire Parasnath Hill, a journey of 54 kilometers (34 mi). The parikrama route is through the forest and is walking as it were.

The temple at Shikharji is another development with a couple segments dating to the eighteenth century. Regardless, the symbol itself is to a great degree old. Sanskrit inscriptions at the foot of the photo date to 1678. At the base of Shikharji is a temple to Bhomiyaji (Taleti). On the dividers of the Jain temple at the town of Madhuban, there is a divider painting depicting each one of the temples on Parjasnath Hill. Temples along the track include:

Ganadhara

In Jainism, the term Ganadhara is utilized to allude the main devotee of a Tirthankara. In samavasarana, the Tīrthankara sat on a position of royalty without touching it (around two crawls above it). Around, the Tīrthankara sits the Ganadharas. According to Digambara custom, just a follower of exceptional brilliance and achievement (riddhi) can completely acclimatize, without uncertainty, hallucination, or confusion, the anekanta teachings of a Tirthankara. The nearness of such a pupil is compulsory in the samavasarana before Tirthankara conveys his sermons. Ganadhara interpret and intervene to other individuals the heavenly stable (divyadhwani) which the Jains assert radiates from Tirthankara's body when he preaches.[15]

The religious sangha of Jainism is partitioned into various orders or troupes called ganas, each headed by a ganadhara. In twentieth century, statues portraying Tīrthankaras and Ganadharas were uncovered in Mayurbhanj district of Odisha

---

[15]Folkert, Kendal W. (1993) *Scripture and Community: Collected Essays on the Jains.* Atlanta: Scholars Press.

2.3 Jainism in Orissa

The stature of Orissa as a place where there is profound spirituality is perceived by the way that it had association with the all the three orthogenetic religious traditions of India- - Hinduism, Buddhism and Jainism. About Jainism in Orissa, it was the 23rd Tirthankara, Parsvanath, who gave the fillip to the tradition and did significant lecturing here in the eighth century BC.

A King named Karakandu of Kalinga built Karakanda Vihar for the spread of Jainism. It is likewise specified that the most famous of 24 Jain Tirthankaras, the last, Vardhaman Mahavira visited the ancient Kalinga capital of Toshali. Buddhism saw a renaissance with Emperor Ashoka, yet Jainism was equally adored[16].

History recounts broad support of Jainism by the Kharavels of the Chedi administration in the first century BC, who grew low-roofed caves in Kumari Parvata- - now known as Khandagiri and Udayagiri- - on the edges of Bhubaneswar, for Jain monks to live in and reflect.

The significant inscriptions inside these caves uncover numerous a certainties of history. They tell about the lords of Chedi line,

---

[16]Foot, Rosemary and Judith Brown (eds.) *Migration: The Asian Experience*London: Macmillan

likewise called Mahameghavanas administering Kalinga around first century BC. The dominant part of these caves originated amid the time of Kharavel, when Jainism was the state religion of Kalinga.

The inscriptions additionally make a specific of other two rulers of this line, Kudeparisi and Vadukha, as the contributors. The records outfit evidence of ambitious career of success of Kharavel, revamping and building of temples and recuperation of Kaling-Jina evacuated by the Nandas of Magadha (fourth century BC) and its installation on the hills by Kharavel.

Indeed, even after the death of lord Kharavel, Jainism kept on holding influence under his successors, the Ganga and the Sailadod administrations excessively treated Jainism with awesome regard - this testified by numerous archeological finds uncovered over the State.

Orissa has allured the religious cluts and groups appropriate from her aged past, regardless of whether for her tribal larger part or her princely commercial base or her soul of osmosis, is truly, precisely not known. The earliest of the off-shoots of Brahmanism, Jainism made its nearness felt in the state as right on time as the seventh century B.C. But for one verifiable stage amid the rule of ahameghavahana King Kharavela, in the first Century B.C., Jainism has truly never been the most mainstream religion of the state. Be that as it may, not at all like its partner, Buddhism, Jainism had never had a brilliant ascent and afterward fall, rather it remained relentlessly well known among certain sections of Society, never experiencing killing. The thorough way of life of the Jains, its syavada reasoning and the idea of ahimsa proceeded to influence certain groups of persevering individuals furthermore, the vendors. Since Jainism, as a confidence, made due as a consistent under current in Orissa since the first century B.C., it has abandoned numerous stays both extrinsic and intrinsic[17].

An investigation of these Jain remains will uncover the legacy of this extraordinary religion. The State of Orissa is a sort of piligrimage to a Jain, as it is to a Hindu. Large portions of the Tirthankaras are related with this state. Rasabhadeva, the principal "Tirthankara, likewise known Jain Heritage of Orissa Indrajeet Mohanty as Adinatha seems to have been worshipped in Kalinga. As indicated by the Jain content, the Avasyaka Nirukti, Sreyansanatha and so on.The eleventh Tirthankara, was born at Simhapura, which was the capital of Kalinga.

The interpretation of the Santi Parva of the Mahabharata by Dr. P.C. Beam - recommends that Aranatha the eighth Tirthankara got goes for Rajapura - a Metropolis of Kalinga. In the previously mentioned Tirthankaras have no recorded validity. They are as yet ambiguous in the fog of myths and legend. Be that as it may, the 22nd and the

---

[17]Foot, Rosemary and Judith Brown (eds.) *Migration: The Asian Experience*London: Macmillan

23rd Tirthankaras are recorded figures. The Khandagiri and Udayagiri sculptures speak to the preachings of Parsvanatha. He exist about 250 a long time before Mahavira i.e. around 850 B.C. The Kumbhakara Jataka, the Uttaradhyayan sutta and the Karakandu Charita discuss Karakandu, the king of Kalinga around seventh - sixth B.C. who was an awesome devotee of Parsvanatha. The Kshetra Samasa, says that Parsvanatha preached at Tamralipti (Tamluk in Bengal) and at Kopakataka (Kupari in Orissa).

The Avasyaka Nirukti proposes that Vardhamana Mahavira preached at Tosali in the eleventh year of his monkhood. This is affirmed by the Vyavahara Bhasya and the Harivamsa Purana. Due to this affiliation of Orissa with these two Tirthankaras at the Kumara and Kumari Parvatas (Khandagiri and Orissa Review * September-October - 2008 Udayagiri), the Jains hold Orissa with incredible significance and reverence. Jainism has been an undercurrent in Orissa's religious development appropriate from the time Parsvanatha preached from the Kumara and Kumari Parvatas to the present day. Kharavela belittled Jainism and made it the state religion in the first Century B.C. The rising notoriety of Buddhism, Saivisim, Saktism and last on Vaisnavism eclipsed Jainism in the accompanying times, in spite of the fact that it kept on being a solid religious constrain among specific sections of society.

The Murunda king Dharmadamodara disparaged Jainism. The Nalas and the Guptas permitted Jainism to prosper in the third fourth Century A.D. The Marathas of the south and the early Ganga kings

42

Daddiga and Madhash acknowledged Jainism. The record of Yuan Chwang talks of the prevalence of Jainism in Orissa in the seventh Century A.D. The Banpur copper plates uncover the anxiety of the Sailodbhavas towards Jainism in the tenth and eleventh hundreds of years A.D. Truly legacy would mean anything that has been transmitted from the past or gave around tradition. One would assume that the stays of the Jain like the stone cut gives in, the temples, sculptures, symbols, books, and works of art and so on are the "legacy" of Jainism. This is, be that as it may, just the extrinsic legacy that we see and esteem. There exists something known as the intrinsic legacy, which we can't see like the influence of Jain reasoning on different factions, on writing, workmanship, society and so on this intrinsic legacy is extremely vital, as it has helped in molding the present Durable culture of our state. Subsequently, just a review of the clear Jain remains won't suffice to compress the legacy of this confidence; additionally a more profound investigation of the culture of the state is required. Like both body and soul make up a living man, both physical and intrinsic stays of Jainism make up a living legacy. Considering the physical stays of Jainism, there is a wealth of sculptures and symbols found all through Orissa.

The hollows at Khandagiri and Udayagiri, with their sculptures what's more, engravings are the earliest remains. Despite the fact that no early Jaina Shrines or monuments, aside from the above, have been found, it is early Jain Hallowed places or monuments, aside from the above, have been found, clearly the extensive quantities of symbols, sculptures, and so on spread around Orissa recommend that there were Jain temples and monuments, which are currently totally broken down. Of the various heterodox groups Jainism as the most accommodative to the Brahmanical religion. In spite of the fact that the Jains did not have faith in the expert of God and that God was the maker, they started to worship the Tirthankaras and a few Gods from the Hindu pantheon[18]. Consequently the Brahmins never truly restricted the Jains and endured it.

The iconographic portrayal of the Jain gods and Brahminical gods is like a layman. In any case, to recognize the Jain from the Brahmanical obligations one ought to pay special mind to recognizing "Signs". These components are the remaining of sitting position of the symbols, the chauri bearers, the kevala tree, flying gandharvas with festoons, champaka check, umbrella, the trifoiled curve and so on and the nakedness of the picture. As Jainism stayed for so long in Orissa, on occasion going to the front line and at different circumstances taking a backbench, it is numerous ways influenced a few different cliques in Orissa. The Jagannatha faction is obligated to Jainism for a large portion of its ceremonies and

---

[18]Forester, Tom (1973) "Pariah Capitalism and Traditional Indian Merchants: Past and Present", pp. 16-36 in Milton Singer, (ed.)

celebrations[19]. Many significant parts of this clique is taken to speak to specific thoughts of Jainism. Additionally Orissa Review September-October - 2008 the Natha faction and the Alekha religion have obtained numerous thoughts from Jainism. Tantric worship moreover has its antecedent in Jainism. Seven Trirthankara figures with seven female figures protected by Ganesa in the Sataghara surrender of Khandagiri and two columns of pictures, the upper story having twenty-four Trithankaras and lower having twenty-four Sasana devi show the female rule being embraced by the Jains. Jain legacy in the field of workmanship and architecture indicate the hollows of Khandagiri and Udayagiri. They were the first to present surrender architecture and engraved excellent sculptures. The Jains seem, by all accounts, to be pioneers in such manner. They likewise may have presented icon worship and construct symbols without precedent for Orissa. The Jains preached their religion in neighborhood lingos like Prakrit, Pali or Ardha-Magadhi. They didn't preach in Sanskrit, yet last on kept in touch with some of their texts in Sanskrit.

---

[19]*Entrepreneurship andModernization of Occupational Cultures in South Asia.* Durham, NC: DukeUniversity Press.

Chapter -3

3.1   The Origin of Jain Temple

A Jain temple is the place of worship for Jains, the followers of Jainism, Derasar is a word utilized for a Jain temple in Gujarat and southern Rajasthan. Basadi is a Jain shrine or temple in Karnataka. The word is for the most part utilized as a part of South India, and additionally in Maharashtra. Its authentic use in North India is saved in the names of the Vimala Vasahi and Luna Vasahi temples of Mount Abu. The Sanskrit word is vasati, it infers an organization including homes of researchers appended to the shrine.

A Vatteluttu inscription discovered from Talakkavu at Putadi near Pulpally reveals the connection of Talakkavu Jain temple with Trikkannamatilakam, which was the most important Jain centre of ancient Kerala. The script and language of the inscription would suggest that the Jain Temples settled here in the 9th -10th centuries of the Christian era. Today we find neither Jains nor Jain temples there.

3.2 Development in Jain Temple Architecture

Jain temples are worked with various building diagrams. Jain temples in North India are entirely unexpected from the Jain temples in South India, which in this manner are extremely not exactly the same as Jain temples in West India. There are two sorts of Jain temples:

Shikar-bandhi Jain temple (one with the vault) and Ghar Jain temple (Jain house temple without arch). All shikar-bandhi Jain temples have many marble segments which are cut magnificently with Demi god act[20]. There is constantly a basic divinity generally called mulnayak in each derasar. The guideline part of Jain temple is called "Gambhara" (Garbha Graha) in which there is the stone cut God icon. One ought to enter the Gambhara without scouring and without wearing puja (revere) articles of clothing. A Jain temple which is more prepared than 100 years and is known as an adventure center is routinely named Tirthaa. The rule god of a Jain temple is known as amula nayak. A Manastambha (area of regard) is a section that is frequently created before Jain temples. It has four 'Moortis' i.e. stone figures of the essential divine force of that temple. One standing up to each traveling: North, East, South and West.

Fig. 3.1:- Jain Tirtha, Shravanabelagola

[20.]Bloomfield, Maurice (1906), <u>A Vedic Concordance: Being an Alphabetic Index to Every Line of Every Stanza of the Published Vedic Literature and to the Liturgical Formulas Thereof</u>

3.3 Religious buildings

3.3.1 Jain Temple

Jain temples are built with various architectural designs. Jain temples in North India are completely different from the Jain temples in South India, which in turn are quite different from Jain temples in West India. There are two type of Jain temples:

i)   Shikar-bandhi Jain temple(one with the dome) and
ii)   Ghar Jain temple (Jain house temple without dome).

All shikar-bandhi Jain temples have many marble pillars which are carved beautifully with Demi god posture. There is always a main deity also known as mulnayak in each derasar. The main part of Jain temple is called "Gambhara" (Garbha Graha) in which there is the stone carved God idol.

A Jain temple which is older than 100 years and is known as a pilgrimage center is often termed a Tirtha.

The main deity of a Jain temple is known as a mula nayak.

3.3.2 Jal Mandir

This is a unique type of temple relates with the Jain Architecture. There are two such examples which is situated in Pawapuri and Nawada. These two temples are based on nagara style of Architecture and surrounded with lake. The jal mandir at pawapuri made of white marble while the jal mandir at Nawada is made of sand stone. The temple is connected by a long bridge from the bank of the surrounding water.

3.3.3 SamosaranTemple

The concept of Samosaran just like Tirthankar-nam-karan is only available in Jainism and not in any other religion.

The creation of samosaran is done by four kinds of Dev (Gods) when a Tirthankar attains Keval Gyan(Complete knowledge). The shape of samosaran is either round or even square. It is of about 8 miles i.e. approx. of 1 yojan. This immensely beautiful development is done so that all and sundry on Earth, sky, water can hear the Tirthankar speech when they attain keval gyan.

Description of samosaran

First Gad (first floor)

The God of wind clears the ground from all the stones, pebbles, thorns, etc., vaiyantra dev make a platform of samosaran out of gold and jewels. Out of the three floors (gad) of Samosaran the first one is prepared by bhuvan pati devta. They prepare it by silver and decorate the borders by gold. To reach this floor there are 10,000 steps from the ground in each four directions. Each step is approximately one hand in width and one hand in height. And here humans and gods who come to hear the Tirthankara keep their vehicles.

Each of the four directions have a door and two gate-mans (dwarpals) are at each door. At one side of these door there is a pond of water. That means, in total, there are four doors in four direction, eight dwarpals two at each door, 40,000 steps and in the first floor of the samosaran.

Second Gad (second floor)

This floor is made by jyotish devta (God of Astrology). This floor is made up of gold and borders are decorated with jewels. To reach this floor there are 5,000 steps each in four directions and just similar to the first step, it has four doors and a pond of water. At the doors of this floor there are goddesses in place of dwarpals at each door. In four corners of this floor there are speacial arrangement and seats (sinhasan) for the Gods to be seated. In this floor birds and animals all sit together forgetting about their enmity. Cat and rat, lion and goat all sit together and go spellbound by the words of the lord. Such is the specialty of this floor.

Third Gad (third floor)

The third floor is prepared by vaiyamanik devta. They prepare this floor with jewels and decorate its borders with Mani. To reach this floor there are 5,000 steps each in four directions and just similar to the first step, it has four doors and a pond of water. At theDoors devtas (Gods) stand in the form of gate-mans. At this part vayantar devta prepare a throne of jewels along with a mat to keep feets. Tirthankar himself come and sit on the throne facing east. As soon Lord takes his place three look-alikes of him automatically take their position in the other three directions. These are basically the idols of his which are created so that everybody feels that they visualizing the ultimate knowledge. At this floor Gods who prepare the sabha, goddesses, sadhu, sadhvis, shravik and shraviks take their place.

The tree under which Tirthankara sit is Ashok Tree, which is about twelve times higher than the height of The Tirthankars. By the sides of the lord, one server carrying a fan made up of cotton threads (Chamar). On top of the head of lord are three inverted umbrellas (chatars). There is enlightened glow on the head of the Lord. He enters from the East and takes tree rounds of the tree and after saying namo tithastakes his seat to the throne.

Lords gives his valuable words twice in a day and each session is 3 hours long. His words are in prakrit language (very old Indian form of dialect). But such is the effect of his words that each and everybody understands it in his or her own language.

This is how a samosaran is created. It is no doubt no more formed because there is no Tirthankara in this part of kal chakra this Ara. But it is still formed in Mahavidya Kshetra where 20 tirthankaras always remain. One can find a look alike of samosaran in every Jain

Mandir made up of silver and being worshiped by the followers of the religion.

3.3.4 Mana-stambhas

Manastambha "section of respect" is a pillar that is regularly developed in front of Jain temples or large Jain statues. In North India, they are bested by four tirthankara images.

As indicated by the Digambara Jain writings like Adi Purana and Tiloyapannati, an immense manastambha remains in front of the samavasarana (divine lecturing hall) of the tirthankaras, which causes somebody entering a samavasarana to shed their pride.

A solid manastambha is a standard element in the Jain temples of Moodabidri. They incorporate a statue of Brahmadeva on the top as a watchman yaksha.

3.4 Important Religious Site

3.4.1 Khandgiri and Udaygiri

Location: 6 Kms from Bhuvneshwar on the West. Secured with the dence forest in the two sides of a tight valley, there are two well-known old hillocks which are essential according to verifiable perspective to be specific - Khandgiri and Udaigiri. Around 200 caves are built on them from the time of Lord Mahaveer to tenth century A. D.

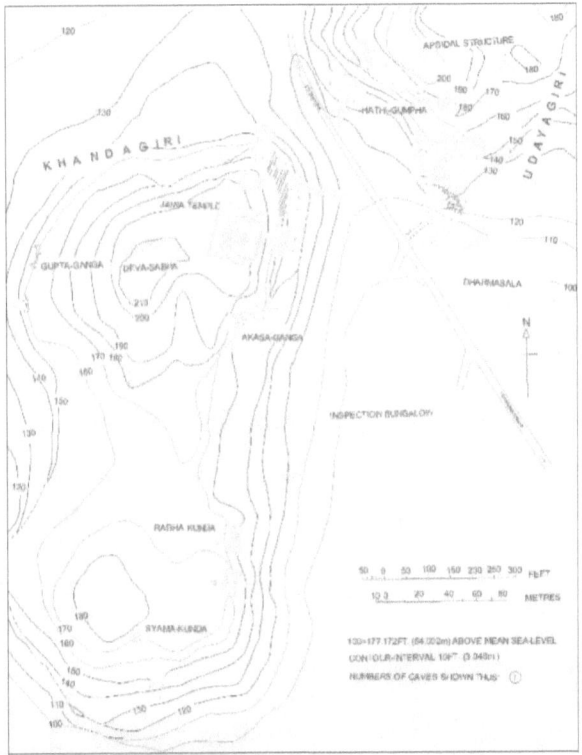

Fig.3.3: - Site Plan Khandgiri and Udaygiri Caves

Khandgiri: There are straight steps to scale on the slope of around 46 Meter high. There are four temples on the mountain. One temple is around 200 years of age. A great many parts are lying behind it. There are eight Khandgasan colonics emblazoned in the cave of King Indrakeshari colosics of Tirthuankars are in Bhagwan Adinath cave. There is one more cave to be specific "Barah Bhuji cave".

Many caves are for contemplation. Akshy Ganga, Gupta Ganga, Shyam kund and Radha kund are behind the principle temple.

Udaigiri: There are many caves amidst second hillock, 35 meter high name Udaigiri. On the entryway of first Alkapuri cave, there are statues of elephants. Behind it, Rani cave has various inner caves. In patel cave there are a few symbols of various Tirthankaras.

The acclaimed Hathi Gupta (Elephantcave) is imperative for its authentic shilalekh. There is a depiction about the Kharvel's triumph of kalingjin on Magadh emperor Pushyamitra. He and his queen had got assembled a colossal temple here. Kharvel likewise masterminded a meeting of Digamber Jain monkish life.

Fig. 3.4:- Hathi Gupta Udayagiri Caves

Among the earliest Jain landmarks are the Udayagiri and Khandagiri Caves, arranged near the city of Bhubaneshwar in Orissa, India. These caves are to some degree typical and generally counterfeit and were cut out as private pieces for Jain clerics in the midst of the rule of King Kharavela of Kalinga (193– 170 BCE). The caves bear etchings and sculptural friezes depicting Tirthankaras, elephants, women, and geese[21].

A large portion of the caves are not characteristic ones but rather are rock cuts and are accepted to have been staying cells and reflection quarters for Jain monks of the time. The monks are accepted to have lived here under unforgiving conditions but then have possessed the capacity to produce dazzling and unpredictable figures delineating the royalty, courts, religious symbols, and customary existence of society. It is a standout amongst the most went by vacation spots of eastern India.

---

[21].*Bhargava, Gopal K. (2006),* Land and People of Indian States and Union Territories: In 36 Volumes. Orissa, Volume 21, *Gyan Publishing House,* ISBN 9788178353777

Fig.3.5:-Rani Gupha, Udaygiri Caves

3.4.2 Khajuraho Jain Temple

During the period of Chandela rule, Jain communities were flourished in Khajuraho region. A number of Jain temples have still existing in this region constructed during this period.Most of the temples constructed during 10-11th century except Ghantai temple built around 960 AD. All these temples are part of UNESCO world heritage site.

Fig. 3.6:- Parshvanath Temple in Khajuraho

3.4.3 Dilwara Jain Temple

Dilwara Jain Temples known for its extraordinary architecture and marvelous marble stone carvings. From outside the temples seems very simple but inside of temple is very richly ornmented. These temples were constructed during 11th to 16^{th}century. The marble ornamentation work of temple is unique and distinct. Every minute details of column and ceiling of temple is just amazing.

The Dilwara Temple complex is consist of five temples dedicated to five Jain trithankaras. The first Temple is dedicated to Shri Mahaveer Swami the 24th Tirthankara. This temple is relatively small. It is constructed in 1582 A.D. The second temple is dedicated to Sri Adi Nath SwamiJi –the first Jain trithankar and known as Vimal Vasahi Temple. This temple is built by Vimal Shah in 1031 A.D. and oldest among all the templex of the complex. The temple has an open courtyard surrounded by corridors all beautifully decorated with marble carved stones. Cells inside this temple are contain tiny images of Jain saints artistically carved on marble stone minutely. The internal dome is aesthetically decorated with design's of flowers and petals, the huge hall of the temple pillars decorated with the carving work of female figures playing musical instruments. The temple also have the "Guda Mandapa" - A simple hall decorated with the images of Shri Adi Nath. The third temple is Shri ParshavNath Temple. This temple was built by Mandika clan in 1459 A.D., It has the tallest shrine along with four big Mandapa's amongst all dilwara temples. Architecturally the carving on the pillars of this temple is supurb. The forth temple is Shri Rishabdaoji Temple. The most of the statues of this temple are built using 'Pittal' (Brass Metal) therefore this temple is also known as Pittalhari/Peethalhar temple. The fifth temple is NemiNathJi Temple or Luna Vasahi Temple - This temple was built in 1230 A.D. by two brothers Tejpal and Vastupal, this temple is dedicated to 22nd saint of Jainism - Shri Nemi Nathji. This temple has one hall named Rag Mandapa which having three hundred and sixty (360) tiny idols of Jain trithankar all minutely crafted on marble.[22].

[22.] *http://www.mountabu.com/tourist_attractions/dilwara_jain_templ e.html visited on 08/01/2018*

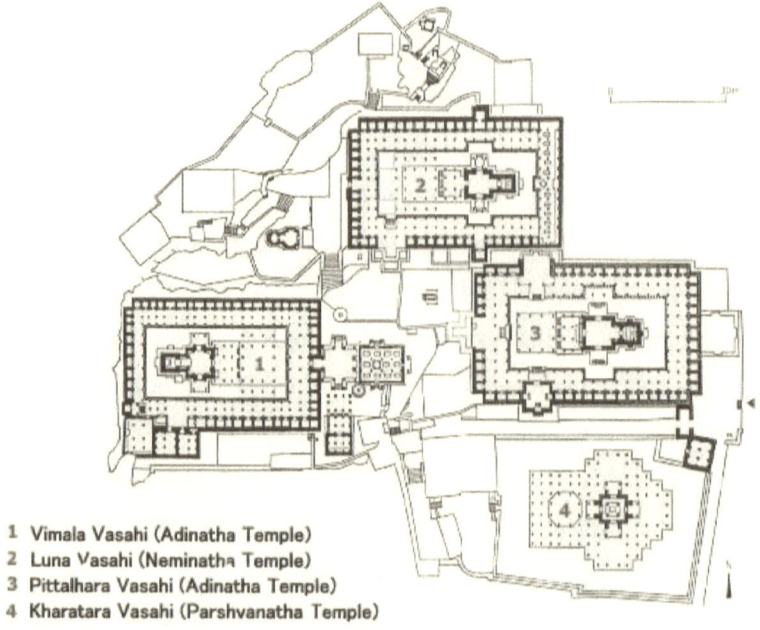

1 Vimala Vasahi (Adinatha Temple)
2 Luna Vasahi (Neminatha Temple)
3 Pittalhara Vasahi (Adinatha Temple)
4 Kharatara Vasahi (Parshvanatha Temple)

Fig. 3.7:- Dilwara Temple site plan

Fig 4.4:- Domed ceiling detail: This image shows the interior of a richly carved marble dome in the Dilwara Temple complex representing Jain Tirthankaras.

Fig 3.8:- Intricately marble carved Pillared hall

3.4.4 Ranakpur Jain Temple

Ranakpur Temples are acclaimed world-wide for their intricate and superb architectural style. It is located in Desuri tehsil near Sadri town in the Pali district of Rajasthan. The construction is well documented in a 1437 CE copper-plate record.It is Built by Seth Dharna Sah with the aid from Rana Kumbha. The principal diety is Lord Adinatha.Ranakpur temples are known for being the largest and most important temples of the Jain cult.

Fig 3.9:- Front view of Ranakpur Jain temple

3.4.5 SonagiriJain Temple

Sonagiri which literally means, "The Golden Peak" is a place sacred to Digambar Jains. It is located on the hill in Datia district of Madhya Pradesh since 9th & 10th Century.this place is popular among devotees and ascetic saints to practice for self discipline and austerity. There are 77 beautiful Jain temples are located on the hills and 26 temples are in the village. Temple's principal deity is Lord Chandraprabhu, 11 feet in height.

Fig 3.10:- **SonagiriJain Temple**

3.4.6Gomateshwara Temple

Fig 3.11:- **Bahubali Statue**

It is one of the largest monolithic statues in the world situated at Shravanabelagola in the Hassan district of Karnataka. The height of statue is 57 feet (17 m) and 26 feet wide. It is built by the Ganga dynasty minister and commander Chamundaraya in 10th century AD.

On August 5, 2007, the statue was voted by Indians as the first of Seven Wonders of India.

On the occasion of Mahamastakabhisheka an event once in 12 years, thousands of pilgrims, devotees and tourists from all over the world flock to the statue.

3.4.7 Sri Sudarshan Kamaldah Ji Temple, Patna

The ancient Jain temple complex is arranged close Gulzarbagh railway station. It is thought to be most seasoned Jain complex in Patna. The temple is committed to the well-known Jain holy person Sundarshan Swami. The temple is known as Shri Shresthi Sundarshan temple or famously Kamaldah Ji[23]. There is tomb of Jain holy person Sthulabhadra. The little shrine contains the impression of the holy person, with Sthulibhadra Charnam composed on it in Devanagari content. Michael Wood of BBC in his narrative on India 'The Story of India' has related the place to the season of Chandragupta Maurya of the Mauryan administration. There is an engraving which gives subtle elements of development

---

[23.]Location of Gulzarbagh - Falling Rain Genomics

of the temple. According to it, the temple is about 200-years of age. The Shitala Mata temple (Agam Kuan) lies west to the Jain shrine.

There are two group of Jain temple isolated by Gulzarbagh railway station. The primary group is arranged on the principle street of Gulzarbagh railway station, named as Sri Digambar Jain Kamaldah Ji Siddha-Kshetra. Here in a little temple, the dark statue of Lord Neminath is found. This temple and the complex is of late birthplace.

The principle Kamaldah Jain temple lies on the opposite side of the Gulzarbagh railway station. It involves two temples. One of the temples is arranged on a mound while other is on the plain (see above photograph). The temple on mound is named as Shri Sthulbhadra Sadhana Sthal (Meditation Center), while temple on the plain is named as Shri Shreshthi Sudarshan Mandir. The entire range is detached and gives a town look agricultural fields all around. The temple complex is spread in a region of 5.04 acres. It is being kept up by Patna Group of Jain Svetambhar Temples Committee.

Fig 3.12:- Sri Sudarshan Kamaldah Ji Temple, Gulzarbagh

3.4.8 Jal Mandir in Pawapuri, Nalanda

The Jal Mandir importance Water Temple, otherwise called Apapuri, in Pawapuri, which means a town without sins, in the Indian territory of Bihar, is a profoundly venerated temple devoted to Lord Mahavira, the 24th Thirthankara (religious minister of Jainism) and originator of Jain religion, which denotes the place of his cremation. Mahavira accomplished Nirvana (salvation) in Pawapuri in 528 BC. The temple has been built inside a tank loaded with red shaded lotus flowers. It is said that the temple was built by King Nandivardhan, Mahavira's elder brother. It is one of the five fundamental temples in Pawpuri, where the "Charan Paduka" or foot impression of Mahavira is worshipped[24].

Amid ancient circumstances around 2600 year prior, Pawapuri was the piece of Magadha Kingdom and was called "Madyama Pawa" or "Apawapuri", Ajatshatru, the child of King Shrenik who was one of the best disciples of Lord Mahavira was the King of Magadh amid the lifetime of Mahavir. Amid the rule of Ajatshatru King Hastipal was the King of Pawapuri. At the point when Lord Mahavira came to Pawapuri he remained in King Hospital's "Rajikshala"[25].

Having accomplished omniscience (Kevala-nana) on the bank of Rju-kula and subsequent to lecturing the principle of Jainism through his heavenly voice (divya-dhvani), Lord Mahavira visited over various zones of the nation and propounded the religious tenets. A short time later he achieved Pavapuri and situated himself on a group or unadulterated piece of stone in a recreation center studded with numerous ponds. He didn't move out for two days; and dove in unadulterated meditation (sukla-dhyana). He stopped the mortal curl and turned into a Siddha in the last quarter of the

---

[24.]*Suriji, Acharya Gunaratna (16 March 2013).* A Visit to Shatrunjaya: Journey to the holiest pilgrimage of Jainism. *Multy Graphics.* ISBN 978-81-926607-0-7.

[25.]*Choudhury, Pranab Chandra Roy (1956).* Jainism in Bihar. *I.R. Choudhury.*

evening of the fourteenth day of the dark portion of the long stretch of Kartika.

There are five primary temples in Pawapuri - the Jal Mandir, the Gaon Mandir, the Samosaran, the New Samosaran and another sanctuary worked by Bibi Mehetab umari. Aside from these temples there is a Digambar Jain Mandir close Jal mandir.

The Gaon mandir or the village sanctuary denotes the spot where Lord Mahavira inhaled his last. It is said that this sanctuary was worked by King Nandivardhan, senior sibling of Lord Mahavira.

Jal mandir is a sanctuary amidst a lake blossoming with lotuses. The principle god of the excellent sanctuary is an exceptionally old "Charan Paduka" of Lord Mahavira. It denotes the spot where the mortal stays of Lord Mahavira was incinerated. It is trusted that this sanctuary was worked by King Nandivardhan, senior sibling of Lord Mahavira. Jal Mandir is worked in the shape of "Vimana" and there is a stone extension around 600 feet long crosswise over it from the bank to the sanctuary[26].

Master Mahavira achieved nirvana in a recreation center, close Pavapuri, circuitous which there were many pounds or lakes. At

---

[26.] *Prasad, Jai Ram (1995).* Community Strucure [sic] and Political Development: A Case Study of Pyarepur Village. *Mittal Publications.* ISBN 978-81-7099-601-9.

introduce the site of the nirvana of Mahavira is acknowledged close Bihar-Sherif where a wonderful Jaina sanctuary remains in the focal point of a major lake. This is acknowledged as the tirthaksetra on all hands. Both the organizations, Digambra and Svetambra, have intentionally acknowledged this place as the spot of the nirvana of Mahavira. A marble sanctuary, the Jalmandir, was later worked amidst the tank, where Lord. Mahavira achieved salvation. Another lovely Jain sanctuary of white marble called Samosharan is situated at this place.

Fig.3.13:- Jal Mandir,Pawapuri

3.4.9 Sri Rijubalika Tirtha, Barakar

Shri Rujubalika Teerth situated in Jharkhand is a Jain pilgrimage focus close Barakar town on the banks of Barakar River. The Teerth Kshetra is arranged on Giridih Madhubani Road. The temple is devoted to Lord Mahavira, the 24th Jain Tirthankara.

By virtue of Lord Mahavir's 12 years' exceptional compensation and his accomplishing "Kevalgyan", this place has turned out to be holy. In this stream an antiquated idol of Lord Mahavir of dazzling beauty was found and this idol is at display introduced in the temple.

Legend of Shri Rujubaluka Teerth

The present day Barker River was the "Rujubaluka River" of the antiquated circumstances. It is trusted that this awesome teerth was Rujubaluka. On the ranch of the farmer Shyamak on the bank of this stream under a Shal tree at a promising time of Vijay Muhurta on the tenth day of the splendid portion of the long stretch of Vaishakh Lord Mahavir accomplished omniscience. Along these lines, this is an extremely holy and holy place of Lord Mahavir Swami's achievement of Kevalgyan.

Temple of Shri Rujubaluka Teerth

The Teerth of Shri Rujubaluka Teerth goes back to the antiquated circumstances. It was before an exceptionally rich and prosperous city. Prior, the temple was made by Shri Dhanpat Singh Ji, on the favorable occasion of the 2600th birth commemoration of Lord Mahavir Swami "Impressions in each of the 4 Directions" were introduced in the premises of the Rujubaluka Temple. The temple has been delightfully finished with unpredictable plans. These remain as interesting case of antiquated art and gloat about the abilities of the craftsmen. The dividers and mainstays of the temple are embellished with specimens of old art and paintings. Outside the temple, the Shal tree is in presence.

Deityin Temple of Shri Rujubaluka Teerth

The temple lodging the idol of Lord Mahavira with his impressions in each of the 4 headings is shocking. The idol of the Lord is 15 cm in height and is white in shading. It is situated in a Padmasana pose. The idol has been delightfully cut from a solitary stone and looks exceptionally engaging. The grinning face of the Lord looks extremely quiet and serene. On the left hand side of the Garbagriha, there remains the first red hued idol of the lord that has been found underneath the Rujubaluka River. There are two pictures of holy cows give the idol of the Lord. On the external sanctum of the Garbagriha, another idol of Lord Parshwanatha Ji is introduced.

Fig. 3.14:- Temple of Shri Rujubaluka Teerth

3.4.10 Samed Shikhar, Madhuban, Parashnath

Samed-Shikhar is a standout amongst the most unmistakable pilgrimage among all the Jain pilgrimages situated in eastern India. Out of 24 tirthankaras 20 tirthakaras were taken Moksha from this holy hill. Devotees from India as well as from the whole way across the world are pulled in to this pilgrimage[27].

[27.]Hachette India (25 October 2013). <u>Indiapedia: The All-India Factfinder</u>. Hachette India. <u>ISBN</u> <u>978-93-5009-766-3</u>

Samed-Shikhar Hill is arranged close Madhuban at a height of 4,450 feet from the ocean surface. Madhuban, is a lovely forest

Fig. 3.15:- Site Plan Parashnath hill with location of tonk

encompassed by hills, trees, gardens and normal beauty[28].

Mulnayak: Bhagawan Parshvanath (Bhagawan Shamaliya Parshvanath) is the Mulnayak. His 92 cms high, dark shaded idol in the Padmasana act is situated on the hill.

Apart from the Shree Parshvanath Temple threre are about 33 tonk on the hill belongs to all other Tirthankara and one jal mandir.

[28.]Jain V. "Shikharji." Herenow4u.net 15 April 2011

Bhomiyaji:There is a temple of Bhomiyaji at the foot of the hill i.e Taleti. As indicated by conviction, a visit to Bhomiyaji temple before starting the pilgrimage to Samet-Shikhar encourages devotees to finish their adventure calmly and the idol ensures the enthusiast all through their voyage who appeals to him and evacuates their obstacles.

History Samet-Shikhar is known by a few names like Samet-Shikhar, Shikharji, Parasnath, Samet Shail, Sametachal, Samet Giri, Parshvanath Pahad, Madhuban and so forth.

As per a conviction, a visit to this consecrated place pulverizes awful karma/sins and evacuates inconveniences of the devotees and ads to religious benefits (punya)[29].

[29.]Balfour, Edward *(1885)*, The Cyclopædia of India and of Eastern and Southern Asia, *3rd volume (Commercial, Industrial and Scientific, Products of the Mineral, Vegetable, and Animal Kingdoms, Useful Arts and Manufactures ed.), B. Quaritch, p. 141,* retrieved 2017-10-02

Fig.3.16:-Shree Parashava Nath Ji Temple Samed Shikhar, Madhuban, Parashnath.

3.4.11 Samosaran temple, Palitana, Gujarat

Samosaran temple is built at the foot hills of the Shantrunjaya Hills in the city of temples, Palitana, Gujarat. Samovasaran temple is a modern temple situated at the base of the main temple complex.

Samosaran temple consists of a large figure of Mahavira in the sitting position with feet in crossed position. The idol is decorated with gems, jewels, gold and silver. The main temple of Samosaran has an iconic image of Adinath made up of a fine piece of marble and the eyes of the idol are made up of crystals. In front of the temple there is a quadrangle that has been designed elaborately. Another famous shrine is situated just opposite to the Adishwara temple.

Architecture of the Temple

The temple is composed of marble and consists of halls made up of columns and towers. There are number of openings in the temples that are surrounded by high mounted walls. The floors are also made up of marble and contain tessellated pattern. The interior of the temple is designed and carved intricately; the ceilings of the temple has pattern similar to geometrical laces that have been clustered together to form a canopy.

Fig. 3.17:- Front view Samosaran Temple

3.4.12 Kirti Stambha, Rajasthan

Fig. 3.18:- Kirti Stambha at Rajsthan

Kirti Stambha is a 12th-century tower situated at Chittorgarh fort in Rajasthan, India. The 22 metre high tower was built by a Jain merchant Jeeja Bhagerwala during the reign of Rawal Kumar Singh (c. 1179-1191) for the glory of Jainism.

Bibliography

Balbir (eds) JainaStudies. Delhi: Motilal Banarsidass

Balfour, Edward (1885), The Cyclopædia of India and of Eastern and Southern Asia, 3rd volume (Commercial, Industrial and Scientific, Products of the Mineral, Vegetable, and Animal Kingdoms, Useful Arts and Manufactures ed.), B. Quaritch, p. 141, retrieved 2017-10-02

Bhargava, Gopal K. (2006), Land and People of Indian States and Union Territories: In 36 Volumes. Orissa, Volume 21, Gyan Publishing House, ISBN 9788178353777

Bloomfield, Maurice (1906), A Vedic Concordance: Being an Alphabetic Index to Every Line of Every Stanza of the Published Vedic Literature and to the Liturgical Formulas Thereof

Choudhury, Pranab Chandra Roy (1956). Jainism in Bihar. I.R. Choudhury.

Dutt, R. C. (1908) Civilisation in the Buddhist Age. Calcutta.

Dwivedi, O. P. (1989) World Religions and the Environment. New Delhi: Gitanjali Publishing House.

Dwivedi, R. C. (ed) (1975) Contribution of Jainism. Banaras: Motilal Banarsidass.

Eisenstadt, S. N. (1984) "Dissent, heterodoxy and civilisational Dynamics: some analytical and comparative indications", In Eisenstadt et al, (eds) Orthodoxy, Heterodoxy and Dissent in India. Berlin: Mouton.

Eliade, Mircea (1961) The Sacred and the Profane. New York: Harper and Row.

Eliot, Charles (1962) Hinduism and Buddhism, vol. I. London: Routledge and Kegan Paul.

Entrepreneurship andModernization of Occupational Cultures in South Asia. Durham, NC: DukeUniversity Press

Flügel, Peter (2000) "Protestantische und Post-Protestantische Jaina-Reformbewegungen: Zur Geschichte und Organisation der Sthanakavasi" I. Berliner Indologische Studien 13/14: 37-103.pp.

Flügel, Peter (2003) "The Code of Conduct of the Terapanth Saman Order", South Asia Research 23(1): 7-53.

Flügel, Peter (2006) "Jainism and Society", Bulletin of SOAS 68: 91-112.

Flügel, Peter (ed) (2006) Studies in Jain History and Culture: Disputes and Dialogues. London: Routledge.

Flügel, Peter (2007) "A Short History of Jain Law," Jaina Studies Newsletter, 2: 24-27.F

Flügel, Peter (2008) "The Unknown Lonka: Tradition and the Cultural Unconscious", pp. 181-271, in Caillat, Colette and Nalini

Fohr, Sherry E. (2001) Gender and Chastity: Female Jain Renouncers. Ph.D.Thesis. University of Virginia.

Folkert, Kendal W. (1993) Scripture and Community: Collected Essays on the Jains. Atlanta: Scholars Press.

Foot, Rosemary and Judith Brown (eds.) Migration: The Asian ExperienceLondon: Macmillan

Forester, Tom (1973) "Pariah Capitalism and Traditional Indian Merchants: Past and Present", pp. 16-36 in Milton Singer, (ed.)

Hachette India (25 October 2013). Indiapedia: The All-India Factfinder. Hachette India. ISBN 978-93-5009-766-3

http://www.mountabu.com/tourist_attractions/dilwara_jain_temple.html visited on 08/01/2018

Jain V. "Shikharji." Herenow4u.net 15 April 2011

Prasad, Jai Ram (1995). Community Strucure [sic] and Political Development: A Case Study of Pyarepur Village. Mittal Publications. ISBN 978-81-7099-601-9.

Suriji, Acharya Gunaratna (16 March 2013). A Visit to Shatrunjaya: Journey to the holiest pilgrimage of Jainism. Multy Graphics. ISBN 978-81-926607-0-7.

www.ingramcontent.com/pod-product-compliance
Lightning Source LLC
Chambersburg PA
CBHW020339290526
45785CB00005B/2100